The Secret Life of Seagulls

by Henry Meyerson

A SAMUEL FRENCH ACTING EDITION

NEW YORK HOLLYWOOD LONDON TORONTO

SAMUELFRENCH.COM

Copyright © 2008, 2009 by Henry Meyerson

ALL RIGHTS RESERVED

CAUTION: Professionals and amateurs are hereby warned that *THE SECRET LIFE OF SEAGULLS* is subject to a Licensing Fee. It is fully protected under the copyright laws of the United States of America, the British Commonwealth, including Canada, and all other countries of the Copyright Union. All rights, including professional, amateur, motion picture, recitation, lecturing, public reading, radio broadcasting, television and the rights of translation into foreign languages are strictly reserved. In its present form the play is dedicated to the reading public only.

The amateur live stage performance rights to *THE SECRET LIFE OF SEAGULLS* are controlled exclusively by Samuel French, Inc., and licensing arrangements and performance licenses must be secured well in advance of presentation. PLEASE NOTE that amateur Licensing Fees are set upon application in accordance with your producing circumstances. When applying for a licensing quotation and a performance license please give us the number of performances intended, dates of production, your seating capacity and admission fee. Licensing Fees are payable one week before the opening performance of the play to Samuel French, Inc., at 45 W. 25th Street, New York, NY 10010.

Licensing Fee of the required amount must be paid whether the play is presented for charity or gain and whether or not admission is charged.

Stock licensing fees quoted upon application to Samuel French, Inc.

For all other rights than those stipulated above, apply to: Samuel French, Inc. 45 West 25th Street, New York, NY 10010.

Particular emphasis is laid on the question of amateur or professional readings, permission and terms for which must be secured in writing from Samuel French, Inc.

Copying from this book in whole or in part is strictly forbidden by law, and the right of performance is not transferable.

Whenever the play is produced the following notice must appear on all programs, printing and advertising for the play: "Produced by special arrangement with Samuel French, Inc."

Due authorship credit must be given on all programs, printing and advertising for the play.

ISBN 978-0-573-69726-5 Printed in U.S.A. #29155

No one shall commit or authorize any act or omission by which the copyright of, or the right to copyright, this play may be impaired.

No one shall make any changes in this play for the purpose of production.

Publication of this play does not imply availability for performance. Both amateurs and professionals considering a production are strongly advised in their own interests to apply to Samuel French, Inc., for written permission before starting rehearsals, advertising, or booking a theatre.

No part of this book may be reproduced, stored in a retrieval system, or transmitted in any form, by any means, now known or yet to be invented, including mechanical, electronic, photocopying, recording, videotaping, or otherwise, without the prior written permission of the publisher.

IMPORTANT BILLING AND CREDIT REQUIREMENTS

All producers of *THE SECRET LIFE OF SEAGULLS must* give credit to the Author of the Play in all programs distributed in connection with performances of the Play, and in all instances in which the title of the Play appears for the purposes of advertising, publicizing or otherwise exploiting the Play and/or a production. The name of the Author *must* appear on a separate line on which no other name appears, immediately following the title and *must* appear in size of type not less than fifty percent of the size of the title type.

CHARACTERS

ANNE – Wears attire suitable for the beach through-out the play: bathing-suit, sun-glasses, hat, sandals. Although she is at times wistful and introspectively sad, there is also a sense of youthfulness.

DON – Married to Anne; wears beach attire opening and last scene, otherwise, casual. Tends toward the taciturn, but also can seem vulnerable. Close friends with Jim.

JIM – Friends with Don; attire indicates he spends a lot of time on the golf course. Shows youthful enthusiasm when discussing golf with Don, otherwise angry and defensive with his wife.

SANDY – Married to Jim, close friend of Anne. In beach attire when with Anne, casual attire when with Jim. As opposed to her friend Anne, Sandy tends to view the world through jaundiced eyes.

FRED – A seagull; you can tell by his feathers or any other device to indicate "seagullness."

GEORGE – Another seagull, same age as Fred.

ETHEL – George's wife (she's expecting).

FRED, JR. – Son of George and Ethel (named after Fred).

MABEL – A seagull looking for prospects.

All Seagull roles may be doubled by the four human characters.

PLACE

A beach in Florida; A bar somewhere up North.

TIME

Now.

AUTHOR'S NOTE

Plays that are written in a vacuum generally stay there. To get the play produced or published, the play had better be written with the work and advice of smart, talented actors in smart, talented workshops of the kind I was fortunate enough to find. These included: New Jersey Dramatists (Peter Ernst, Artistic Director), and Times Square Playwrights (Tom Thornton, Artistic Director). I would especially like to thank Jennifer Earhart and Branan Whitehead of New Jersey Dramatists, and Sharlene Hartman and Jim Nugent of Times Square Playwrights. Also, despite their occasional lapse in decorum, I would like to thank the multitude of seagulls for their unstinting encouragement and feathers.

Finally, as always, I dedicate this play to my wife, Ronnie, who has always been the smartest and best looking gull on the beach.

–Henry Meyerson
2009

(SETTING: Two beach chairs, side by side, facing audience.)

(AT LIGHTS: **ANNE** *and* **DON** *enter in bathing suits, sit, apply sun-block to themselves. They sit back and admire the view.)*

ANNE. Florida is beautiful this time of year, isn't it? The blue sky, the blue water, the white sand, the seagulls. Reminds me of our honeymoon. Remember the night when we did it on the beach? I still think that old man saw us. I mean, why else would he have been winking at us the next morning? Now that I think of it, it was more like leering. Yep, he definitely saw us. *(beat)* Bermuda. It was just beautiful. The motorbikes. The crappy English food. Oh, the flowers. I never saw such beautiful flowers. The reds, magentas, blues, yellows. Bright, sparkling almost. And the aroma of those flowers. It's been ten years and I can still smell the aroma. *(beat)* You know I think I still have that kilt you bought. I think it's still up in the attic. Now that your legs have…well, filled out, you might look good in it. *(beat)* No, probably not. *(beat)* Jesus, were we young. *(beat)* I guess all beaches are beautiful if the weather is right. They all have the same sand, the same blue water, the same blue sky. Probably the same seagulls. You know, there might only be a hundred seagulls in the whole world and they just fly from place to place just like us, flying from one beach to another, laying under the same sky, on the same beach, looking at the same sea. Those may be the same seagulls flying over our head right now. *(beat)* Strange isn't it that I've never seen anyone hit with seagull shit. All these years, all these seagulls, I've never seen anyone hit. *(beat)* You know which seagulls are lucky? The ones that are born near garbage dumps. They don't have to go out looking for food like these poor little guys. The food is brought to them. Everyday those seagulls wake up and a new load of food is being trucked in right to their doorstep. Do seagulls have nests or do they just sort of squat down? I guess it's a nest, isn't it. Anyway, all they have to do is walk a few steps and eat their breakfast. If they could read, they'd have the newspaper brought in with their food. Just lucky to be born near a dump. I guess I'm lucky not to have been born near a dump. The smell...whoa! *(beat)* How did I get from the beauty of Bermuda and our honeymoon to the stink of a garbage dump? The mind is a strange animal, Don.

(after a pause)

DON. I'm going.

(Lights fade on **ANNE** *as* **DON** *puts on a shirt and crosses to sit with* **JIM** *at a table in a coffee shop.)*

JIM. You remember the eighth hole on that course.

DON. Dog leg left?

JIM. Right.

DON. I think it's left, Jimmy.

JIM. No, I mean you're right, it's left.

DON. Got ya.

JIM. What, about 310 to the pin, right?

DON. Yeah.

JIM. Reached it with a driver and wedge.

DON. Get out.

JIM. Dropped it pin high.

DON. Get out.

JIM. Knocked it down for a birdy wordy, Donny, baby.

DON. Son of a gun.

JIM. Even better. On the twelfth...

DON. About 515?

JIM. Exactly.

DON. Sand traps.

JIM. Like the fucking Sahara.

DON. So?

JIM. Driver, three wood, nine iron, one putt and gone, baby.

DON. You birdied the twelfth?

JIM. You got it.

DON. Get out.

JIM. Birdy wordy, Donny, baby.

DON. Good going, big guy.

JIM. Yup. Two birdy wordies for the round.

DON. What'd you shoot for the round?

JIM. The whole round?

DON. Yeah. With the two birdies, what'd you shoot?

JIM. 104.

DON. That's not a score, Jimmy, it's a fever.

JIM. Sure, Don, never mind my good holes. You always have to be a downer. I tell you my good stuff, you make sure to bring up my bad.

DON. Just asking.

JIM. Well, sometimes you should lighten up, Donny.

DON. I feel light. Sometimes you ignore the dark side, Luke.

JIM. Very funny.

DON. Just trying to "lighten up."

JIM. You play in Florida?

DON. Yeah.

JIM. How'd you make out, Tiger?

DON. Fine.

JIM. Liar.

DON. Just fine, thank you.

JIM. You're not going to tell, are you?

DON. Not after this little exchange. I'd be like a sitting duck.

JIM. Annie go with you?

DON. Of course.

JIM. She play.

DON. Yup.

JIM. This is like pulling teeth.

DON. You ask, I tell.

JIM. How is Annie?

DON. She tends to slice and not much of a short game.

JIM. How is Annie?

DON. I left her.

JIM. Where?

DON. At the beach.

JIM. Don't blame you. I hate the beach.

DON. I left her.

JIM. Yeah, you said. That's how come you're here.

DON. I mean I left her.

JIM. Left as in left left.

DON. As in bye-bye.

JIM. At the beach.

DON. Staring into the sea and babbling about seagulls shitting on people. After five days of listening to her, I felt staples were being driven into my head.

JIM. You never see that happen, do you?

DON. Of course you don't. The staples thing is just a figure of speech.

JIM. I was talking about the seagulls. Given the number of seagulls at the beach, you'd think you would have seen at least once in a while someone get shat on.

DON. Is that a real word?

JIM. Which?

DON. Shat.

JIM. No idea, but you get the point. Have you heard from her?

DON. Who?

JIM. Anne.

DON. No.

JIM. You haven't spoken?

DON. Not a word.

JIM. You've been married…

DON. Ten years.

JIM. And you just…

DON. No, not just, Jim. Jeez, give me some credit.

JIM. So how long…?

DON. About a week.

JIM. Still sounds like a…

DON. Not a snap decision, Jim. Plenty of thought went into this. *(beat)* Well, maybe not plenty, but enough. It was the fucking seagulls put it over the edge.

JIM. Yeah, I can see that.

(Lights cross fade to:)

(ANNE and SANDY seated in the beach chairs.)

SANDY. Just like that?

ANNE. Exactly. Isn't that strange?

SANDY. I've heard of these things happening.

ANNE. Really?

SANDY. Oh, sure.

(pause)

Well, come to think of it maybe not. Just got up and left, huh?

ANNE. Just got up and left.

SANDY. Without a word.

ANNE. No. Let me think. Ah. He said, "I'm going."

SANDY. "I'm going."

ANNE. That's what he said, Sandy. "I'm going."

SANDY. What did you think he meant?

ANNE. What do you mean?

SANDY. Well, did you think Don meant he'll be right back, or that he was going to the bathroom, or that he was, I don't know, leaving.

ANNE. Leaving as in…?

SANDY. Leaving leaving.

ANNE. I didn't give it much thought at the time. I guess I figured he'd be right back. That he had to tinkle or something. No reason to think otherwise.

SANDY. What were you guys doing?

ANNE. Just sitting here chatting about the beach, the sky, the water and about our honeymoon. I thought it was a nice romantic time. Then he said "I'm going" and then he left.

SANDY. A week ago.

ANNE. Tomorrow will be a week. Strange, don't you think?

SANDY. That Don left or that you waited a week to call anyone?

ANNE. That he left.

SANDY. But why did you wait so long to call?

ANNE. I told you. I thought he was coming back.

SANDY. Annie, it's been a week.

ANNE. Tomorrow.

SANDY. What have you been doing for the past week in this hotel alone?

ANNE. Waiting.

(cross fade to:)

DON. Where's Sandy?

JIM. Not sure. When I got back a couple of days ago from the golfing thingee, she wasn't here.

DON. Ah. You thought she would be home, then.

JIM. No reason to think otherwise, right? I mean she's always been home when I got there.

DON. Didn't she go with you on this trip?

JIM. Yeah.

DON. So…

JIM. I was putting out the seventh hole, turned around and she was gone. When I got back to the room she was gone. I just figured she'd gotten bored and went home.

DON. So what did you do?

JIM. Finished out the week-end. Beautiful course.

DON. Yeah, I remember.

JIM. Two birdy wordies.

DON. She leave a note?

JIM. No.

DON. Well, at least we know she's not with her mother.

JIM. How do we know that?

DON. Isn't her mother dead?

JIM. Oh, that's right. Boy, that old lady hated me.

DON. Why's that?

JIM. She thought I played too much golf. Apparently her ex-husband played a lot of golf.

DON. That would be Sandy's…

JIM. No. That was her step-father. Her father just disappeared one day.

DON. How do you disappear?

JIM. Way Sandy tells it, he left the house to buy some cough drops and never came home.

DON. So there was no note?

JIM. From her father?

DON. No, Sandy.

JIM. Nope.

DON. Anything missing?

JIM. Some of her clothes.

(cross fade to:)

ANNE. It is nice here, isn't it?

SANDY. So restful.

ANNE. Quiet.

SANDY. Except for the seagulls.

ANNE. What's wrong with the seagulls.

SANDY. All that squawking. *(makes squawking sound)* Sounds eerie at night. *(makes squawking sound)*

ANNE. For some reason I find that sound reassuring.

(pause)

SANDY. I left him.

ANNE. Who?

SANDY. Jim.

ANNE. I assumed that when you got off the plane without him.

SANDY. You knew I left Jim?

ANNE. He's not here, is he? So, yeah, I figured you left him when you came down here.

SANDY. I don't mean I just left him. I left left him.

ANNE. Left left?

SANDY. As in adios, Jimmy, baby.

ANNE. Why?

SANDY. Golf. Golf, golf, golf. Endless playing, then endlessly talking about it.

ANNE. Is that a good enough reason to leave your husband?

SANDY. It was for me, kiddo.

ANNE. What did he say?

SANDY. I told you. He was talking about golf.

ANNE. I mean when you told him you were leaving.

SANDY. Since I didn't tell him I was leaving, not much he could have said.

ANNE. You just up and left?

SANDY. Between the seventh and eighth holes.

ANNE. Just like Don. Not a word, up and left.

SANDY. Except no seagulls.

(cross fade to:)

*(**FRED**, a seagull, is squatting on the stage. **GEORGE**, a seagull, enters, walks around then approaches **FRED**.)*

GEORGE. Is this seat taken?

FRED. Plenty for everyone, pal.

GEORGE. I'm George.

FRED. Pull up some sand, George. I'm Fred.

*(**GEORGE** squats. He makes seagull noises as he makes himself comfortable. They both preen their feathers for awhile.)*

FRED. *(cont.) (upbeat)* Nice out here today, right George? The sea, the sand, the sky, bright sun. Makes you glad to be a seagull.

GEORGE. It certainly does.

FRED. *(downbeat)* Then again it's pretty much the same all over isn't it. Seen one beach, seen 'em all. Kind of desolate out here sometimes. Sometimes the fog rolls in can't see your beak in front of your wing.

GEORGE. I wouldn't know.

FRED. You must have seen other beaches.

GEORGE. Nope.

FRED. Ah, you're one of those land-locked seagulls. This must be quite a change.

GEORGE. And a pleasant one, that's for sure.

FRED. Welcome to paradise, George.

GEORGE. Thanks. And you're right, Fred. It is lovely here.

FRED. Here on holiday or business?

GEORGE. Just taking a little vacation. First ever.

FRED. That right? First land-locked, now never been away. You've been under wraps, George.

GEORGE. Oh, it's been fine. You get born into something that works, pretty much okay to stick to it.

FRED. Maybe so. Here with the misses?

GEORGE. No. She's not much for long trips, so I just took off, so to speak.

FRED. You've really never just flown the coop?

GEORGE. Nice play on words, Fred, but nope, pretty much stay home with the misses.

FRED. Where's home?

GEORGE. Up north. Staten Island.

FRED. No kidding? What a great place.

GEORGE. You've been there?

FRED. I'm a travelin' gull, George. Yeah, I've been there a couple of times. Are you close to the landfill?

GEORGE. Close? I'm right at the landfill.

FRED. In?

GEORGE. On. Like the house on a lake or on a golf course.

FRED. That is awesome.

GEORGE. Yes. A lovely spot. Great view. I get to see the garbage trucks come in and unload.

FRED. That must be exciting.

GEORGE. It's a comfortable life.

FRED. That spot must have cost you a pretty penny.

GEORGE. I made some good investments in garbage recycling. I just kept trading up.

FRED. Sweet.

GEORGE. How about yourself? Vacation?

FRED. Kind of. I'm single so, like I said, I just keep moving around. Wanderlust, you might say. Right now I have a little bachelor pad on the other side of the dune over there.

GEORGE. Very nice.

FRED. Over all, yeah, but I don't have your luxury. I have to either go get my own food or call in.

GEORGE. You have call in?

FRED. I usually order week old sushi.

GEORGE. Very nice. If I'm lucky, sometimes I find some of that.

FRED. I wouldn't complain. You've got a smorgasbord of stuff right at your door.

GEORGE. It's not all week-old sushi, Fred. It may be delivered to the door, but it's seagull eat seagull out there to get the stuff.

FRED. Competition, huh?

GEORGE. Almost enough to make me a vegetarian.

FRED. So, you have a great, stable location, but have to fight to feed. I have unlimited freedom to move around, but hope to get dead fish washed up on the beach each day for my meals.

GEORGE. Are you comparing our lives?

FRED. Just our situations.

(cross fade to:)

ANNE. Do you think Jim knows you've gone away?

SANDY. Since I didn't tell him, he probably hasn't even noticed.

ANNE. Oh, he must have noticed. After a while he'd notice.

SANDY. Took you a week. Don goes for a pee, doesn't come back for a week and you figure he was going for the world record for taking the longest leak in history.

ANNE. I knew he was gone, Sandy. I just didn't realize he had gone gone. There's a difference. I asked if you think Jim noticed you had gone or had gone gone.

SANDY. A distinction without a difference.

ANNE. I don't know what that means.

SANDY. It means Jim just doesn't give a shit either way.

ANNE. Oh, I don't believe...

SANDY. It all became perfectly clear to me on the seventh hole.

ANNE. What did?

SANDY. He was putting out or digging a divot or whatever and I just realized he would rather be doing that than be with me.

ANNE. Excuse me, Sandy, but a lot of woman are golf widows.

SANDY. And a lot of women are schmucks, Anne. Ten years of trailing him around the country, course by course, hole by hole, divot by divot. Enough. Enough "Where'd the fucking ball go?" Enough watching him throw the clubs into the pond. And more than enough, thank you, of "birdy wordy."

ANNE. What?

SANDY. He says that sometimes when he's playing and it seems to make him very happy.

ANNE. *(puzzled)* Birdy wordy. What do you think it means?

SANDY. Am I attractive?

ANNE. Well...

SANDY. Am I attractive!

ANNE. Yes.

SANDY. Would men find me appealing?

ANNE. Sure.

SANDY. Do I have a right to determine my future?

ANNE. Of course.

SANDY. Then no more birdy wordies, Anne. Never again.

ANNE. Can't say I blame you.

SANDY. Blame me? I should be applauded for putting up with him for so long. I was just up to here *(touches her throat)* with him. Fed up.

ANNE. Do you think that's why Don walked out?

SANDY. Birdy wordies?

ANNE. Being fed up with me.

SANDY. Yes.

ANNE. You didn't have to answer so quickly. You could have thought about it a bit first.

SANDY. Why beat around the bush. Fed up with you. That's it. Just as I was fed up with Jim.

ANNE. But what was there to be fed up about?

(SANDY stares at ANNE.)

But we loved each other.

SANDY. I love profiteroles, but that doesn't mean…

ANNE. What's that?

SANDY. What?

ANNE. Profit something. What you just said.

SANDY. Profiteroles?

ANNE. Yeah, that.

SANDY. Pastry filled with cream.

ANNE. That sounds good.

SANDY. You usually pour chocolate syrup over them.

ANNE. Wow.

SANDY. Can I get back to…

ANNE. I'm sorry, but I always like to learn.

SANDY. But somehow we went from doomed marriages to profiteroles.

ANNE. You think they're doomed?

SANDY. Doomed, doomed, doomed. Kaput. Dead. They've passed on! These marriage are no more! They have ceased to be! They have expired and gone to meet their maker! They're a stiff! Bereft of life, they rest in peace! Their metabolic processes are now history. They are off the twig! They have kicked the bucket, shuffled off this mortal coil, run down the curtain and joined the choir invisible!! THESE ARE EX-MAR-RIAGES!! *(pause)* Did you recognize the Parrot Sketch from Monty Python? I love Monty Python, don't you.

ANNE. Not really, no.

SANDY. There's your problem.

ANNE. Not liking Monty Python?

SANDY. Having no sense of humor. There are times you are a stick in the mud, Anne.

ANNE. I am not.

SANDY. You are. A. Stick. In. The. Mud.

ANNE. And that's why Don left?

SANDY. I have no idea why Don left.

ANNE. So it might have been for other reasons.

SANDY. It might. But that doesn't mean you aren't a stick in…

ANNE. Alright. I get it. The question is what to do now. I can't continue to live here in a hotel.

SANDY. Sure you can. It's on old Donny Wonny's credit card, isn't it?

ANNE. Oh, I can't…

SANDY. Oh, sure you can.

ANNE. You are a devil.

SANDY. Shall we order some food and drink.

(cross fade to:)

DON. You miss her?

JIM. Sandy?

DON. Yeah.

JIM. It's only been a couple of days.

DON. Still…

JIM. You miss Anne?

DON. I'm not sure. I mean, there are things I don't miss and things I do.

JIM. This isn't like an all-time hit list, Donnie. You gotta take the whole package.

DON. She just makes me nuts with her…I never told anyone this, Jim, but I think Anne is a little dim upstairs.

JIM. So?

DON. Well, the things she says sometimes don't make a lot of sense.

JIM. Sandy says the same thing about me.

DON. That you're dim upstairs?

JIM. That I make her crazy sometimes.

DON. You seem okay to me.

JIM. That's because we talk about golf.

DON. Exactly my point. You and I share an interest. Anne talks about seagulls and beaches and bird shit. I'm sitting there listening to her and thinking who the fuck cares.

JIM. That's all she talks about? Seagulls and beaches?

DON. I'm just using that as an example.

JIM. So, when you're with her, what do you want to talk about?

DON. Nothing, really. I'm just kind of there, you know. Sitting and listening.

JIM. So she's like elevator music.

DON. No, I happen to like elevator music. Sometimes she's more like a small jack hammer banging into my brain.

JIM. And all you want is peace and quiet.

DON. Exactly. Jimmy, you just nailed it. Peace and quiet. That's it.

JIM. Maybe that's why Sandy left me.

DON. You're not a noisy guy. If anything…

JIM. No, because that's what I want, too.

DON. Peace and quiet?

JIM. That's why I play golf. Out there in the sun, on the green grass, just me the ball and the club. Nice, you know.

DON. Where do you think she went?

JIM. Sandy?

DON. Yeah.

JIM. Haven't a clue.

DON. Think she'll be back?

JIM. Haven't a clue.

DON. The whole thing is strange.

JIM. You mean Sandy?

DON. The whole thing.

JIM. You going back to Anne?

DON. Haven't a clue, Jimmy.

JIM. Strange, huh?

(cross fade to:)

SANDY. That was good, but I ate too much again, as usual. Did you ever see so many shrimp?

ANNE. I never saw anyone eat so many shrimp.

SANDY. I felt like a great white.

ANNE. Great white what?

SANDY. Great white Sandy, is what. I think I'm sick.

ANNE. Maybe I shouldn't have had so many piña coladas. I'm a little tipsy.

SANDY. You needed to unwind, Anne. This has been a brutal week for you. I don't remember these pants being so tight.

ANNE. It must be brutal for you, too.

SANDY. No biggie. I'll go on a diet when I get back home.

ANNE. I meant leaving Jim.

SANDY. I think it's tougher for the leavee than the leaver. At least in my case. Better to act than be screwed.

ANNE. You think I was screwed?

SANDY. Like a forty watt bulb.

ANNE. Did you screw Jim?

SANDY. That's been part of the problem.

ANNE. That you screwed him?

SANDY. That I didn't. The golf wiz is more consumed with birdy wordies than with sexy wexies.

ANNE. I've got the same problem with Don.

SANDY. No sexy wexy?

ANNE. It's like he suddenly took vows, for Christ sake.

SANDY. Yeah, that's who you take vows for.

ANNE. What?

SANDY. You take vows for Christ's sake.

ANNE. I was trying to make a joke.

SANDY. I know. So was I.

(Both start getting the giggles.)

ANNE. I'm tipsy on piña coladas. You're tipsy on shrimp.

SANDY. You think shrimp will ever be a good substitute for sexy wexy?

ANNE. They will if you do it right.

(laughing harder)

SANDY. Oh, Anne, you are bad.

ANNE. Not yet, but the night is young.

SANDY. I'm putting you to bed before you get into any trouble.

ANNE. I love you, Sandy, but not in that way.

SANDY. Too many drinks can spoil the girl.

ANNE. Here's hoping.

SANDY. You really having sex issues with Don?

ANNE. More like no sex issues.

SANDY. We're both married to duds, Anne.

ANNE. I can't help but think it's my fault.

SANDY. Well, I can tell you for sure it is my fault. Now that's a secret just between us girls.

ANNE. I thought you said it was because he was so interested in golf.

SANDY. It is now. That's because I slowly made myself less and less appealing and showed less and less interest. I eat, he golfs.

ANNE. Or maybe he golfs, you eat.

SANDY. Whatever.

ANNE. No, this is important, Sandy.

SANDY. For me or for you?

ANNE. Both of us.

SANDY. But I'm not interested in looking deeper.

ANNE. Okay, then for me. Who started the cycle, you or Jim?

SANDY. How the fuck do I know?

ANNE. Tell me and I'll buy you more shrimp.

SANDY. You sure know how to woo a girl, Annie. Okay. Imagine two boats in the water.

ANNE. You're not answering the question. Who started the cycle, Sandy?

SANDY. I am answering it. Just be quiet.

ANNE. Is this a metaphor?

SANDY. I think it's an analogy.

ANNE. What's the difference?

SANDY. I don't know.

ANNE. Go ahead.

SANDY. The boats are tied together.

ANNE. Okay.

SANDY. Then they get untied.

ANNE. Okay.

SANDY. Then they drift apart.

ANNE. I think I'm following you.

SANDY. Which boat drifted first, Anne?

ANNE. You're comparing you and Jim to boats?

SANDY. I'm comparing the situations.

ANNE. Drifting implies indifference.

SANDY. Right. Very good. I'm indifferent.

ANNE. How is that possible after ten years?

SANDY. I guess it's just something I'm capable of.

ANNE. I don't believe that.

SANDY. It's true.

ANNE. Remember in high school, you and me and Carol were close.

SANDY. I'm old, but not senile. Of course I remember. What does that have to do with boats?

ANNE. Remember when Carol died?

SANDY. Like it was yesterday.

ANNE. We cried, Sandy. For weeks, we cried.

SANDY. I think about her and I still cry. So?

ANNE. I know everyone thinks I'm a little slow, Sandy, and maybe I am, but as I see it boats don't have desires or needs. They're boats. Wood, steel, whatever. They don't feel. We've been friends long enough for me to know you feel. So don't give me this baloney about just drifting away like a couple of boats. You and Jim aren't boats. What happened?

SANDY. I don't know what caused the drift, Anne. What I do know is that we became untied.

ANNE. *(resigned)* Have it your way. *(clearly changing the subject)* So…no sex.

SANDY. I wasn't lying before, Anne. I wasn't being coy. I really don't know what happened.

ANNE. I believe you. That's why I moved on. So…no sex.

SANDY. I don't even know how to find out what happened.

ANNE. Yeah, I get it, Sandy. So…no sex.

SANDY. Correct that. I don't know if I want to find out what happened.

ANNE. Talking to you, I think I'm beginning to understand what about me was bothering Donny. So…no sex.

SANDY. So…who said anything about no sex.

ANNE. You did.

SANDY. I said no sex with old Jimbo. I never said no sex.

ANNE. *(whispers)* Vibrator?

SANDY. You could call it that, except this one has real blood in it.

ANNE. Oh, I don't believe…you would never…Really?

SANDY. Beats the hell out of using shrimp, my dear.

ANNE. You never told me.

SANDY. Nothing I'm proud of. *(beat)* Well, yes I am, matter of fact.

ANNE. Who?

SANDY. No one you know. Do you realize how hard it is to find a man who doesn't play golf?

ANNE. Was that the only criterion?

SANDY. And breathing. That's about it. Breathing and no golf. But, really, the no golf was the tough part.

ANNE. How long?

SANDY. Excuse me.

ANNE. *(laughing)* I meant in time. *(beat)* Well, okay, how long that way, too.

SANDY. Long enough in all ways, my dear.

ANNE. How does it work?

SANDY. Excuse me again, Anne. Those piña coladas are knocking you silly.

ANNE. Now you are being evil. You know what I meant.

SANDY. He calls my cell phone. We meet. We go somewhere.

ANNE. Amazing.

SANDY. Not really. People do it all the time.

ANNE. Amazing you, my best friend, you do this. Don't you think it's amazing?

SANDY. Mostly I think it's sad.

(cross fade to:)

GEORGE. So, comparing our situations, how do we stack up?

FRED. I know other bird's lives seem better than one's own, but…

GEORGE. The sand is always cleaner kind of thing?

FRED. Yeah. But here you are, a family man…

GEORGE. No, not quite.

FRED. Oh, I thought you had chicks.

GEORGE. Bad luck there. Couple of eggs cracked.

FRED. Sorry to hear it.

GEORGE. Well, given the gestation period is only a couple of weeks, no biggie. My wife will just lay a couple of more.

FRED. See, that's it. You are optimistic about the future. Got your nest, little plot of ground, wife, food plan and now planning a family. You got all your people in a row, George.

GEORGE. Yeah, I guess I am pretty lucky.

FRED. Me, on the other hand…

GEORGE. Fred, I'll bet you are a happy go lucky gull. Don't like your deal, take to the air, ride the currents, see the sights. Part of me is envious.

FRED. I appreciate the support, George, but let's face it. I'm pushing seven. Got, what, maybe another three, five years tops. I can feel it in my wings. One day I'll dive for a herring and never come up.

GEORGE. You surprise me, Fred. Granted we've only just met, but I took you for a devil-may-care kind of gull. Beach bum and lovin' it. Now you sound really bummed out, depressed like.

FRED. We've learned to hide it well, but I think depression runs in the family, George. My father kept playing dodge with the fishing fleet until he finally got tangled up in the netting. My grandmother beak-dived into a cruise ship.

GEORGE. The dark side of being a seagull.

FRED. Same kind of stories on my mother's side.

GEORGE. How sad. Where there any signs before…

FRED. No, just a lot of staring off into the horizon.

GEORGE. All seagulls do that, Fred.

FRED. Oh, you're right. Then, no, no signs.

GEORGE. Are you…?

FRED. Looking to get my feathers flattened? Not yet, but then there's all this aimlessness I feel. Flying here, floating there. Just drifting, you know?

GEORGE. But we all tend to do that, too.

FRED. Yeah, that's true, too. Okay, how about this? I wish I were different. I don't want to be Fred the seagull anymore.

GEORGE. Who do you want to be?

FRED. Fred the dog.

GEORGE. Dog? You mean those stupid four legged earth-bound dorks that keep chasing us around the beach?

FRED. They all seem so care-free. They frolic. I want to frolic, George. I want to chase things. Dogs look like they have fun. I want to have fun.

GEORGE. My wife and I have fun just being seagulls. Sometimes we fly over shopping malls and do the dive bombing bit. Splat. *(laughs)* Splat. Terrific fun. Ever try that?

FRED. I used to. I'll grant you the first hundred times or so I shat on someone it was a blast, but, I don't know, the thrill is gone.

GEORGE. Is that a word?

FRED. Which?

GEORGE. Shat. I don't think there is a past tense of shit.

FRED. Do you teach school, George?

GEORGE. Sorry.

FRED. Do you understand what I'm saying?

GEORGE. That you're jaded, bored with your life.

FRED. Exactly. That's why I want to change, to become a dog.

GEORGE. Can you live with the fact that what you want is impossible to achieve?

FRED. You're saying I can't become a dog?

GEORGE. I'm saying it's a low order of probability.

(cross fade to:)

ANNE. Sad is certainly better than indifferent. Maybe you should talk to someone.

SANDY. I am.

ANNE. Me?

SANDY. Of course. And the best part is, if I keep feeding you piña coladas, you won't remember a thing.

ANNE. Your being sad makes me sad.

SANDY. Do I seem sad to you?

ANNE. Not really.

SANDY. I never said I was sad. What's sad is "it." Other than that, I'm fine.

ANNE. And the "it?"

SANDY. My life, sweetie. My ever lovin', headin' down the drain life.

ANNE. So it's your life that's sad, not you.

SANDY. Right.

ANNE. Is that what you called a distinction without a difference?

SANDY. Maybe in your mind. In my mind there is a clear difference.

ANNE. That's so sad.

SANDY. That's the piña colada talkin'.

ANNE. That's your friend of…how many years is it?

SANDY. Enough to know when it's you and when it's piña colada.

ANNE. Well, I insist on being sad about both you and your life which, if I may say so, is even sadder than me and mine.

SANDY. How do you, in your alcohol addled little brain, arrive at that?

ANNE. Because my husband doesn't say birdy wordy, that's why.

SANDY. You may be right. I had to live with it for ten years.

ANNE. I'm not as strong as you.

SANDY. Of course you are. You sat here a week toughing it out all by your little lonesome.

ANNE. Toughing it out? This is a first class hotel on a beautiful beach, Sandy. I have all these pitchers of piña coladas. I can't take credit for being tough.

SANDY. Ever live by yourself, Anne?

ANNE. No.

SANDY. Went from living with your parents to living with Donny, right?

ANNE. Yes.

SANDY. Who'd you live with this past week.

ANNE. Just me.

SANDY. Did you pick up anyone?

ANNE. No.

SANDY. Flirt?

ANNE. No.

SANDY. Lust after one of the beach guys?

ANNE. No.

SANDY. Doesn't that show strength?

ANNE. It shows fear and maybe a little stupidity and a lot of repression. But strength? I don't see it.

SANDY. Then I think you need to go talk to someone.

(cross fade to:)

FRED. Just because we're gulls doesn't mean we have to take what's given us.

GEORGE. Well, I agree with some of that. We can improve our lives, but becoming a dog is a little out there, Fred.

FRED. I refuse to settle for the status quo.

GEORGE. There are some things you can change, some you can't and you have to learn to understand the difference.

FRED. Isn't that part of AA.

GEORGE. Abalone Anonymous. That's right. I was an addict, Fred. Just couldn't get enough.

FRED. Even though you knew how fattening abalone are and the harm it might do, how the extra weight would screw up your ballast.

GEORGE. Oh, I knew, but I was hooked up to my pin feathers. Then, of course, I couldn't stop at abalone. I had to move on.

FRED. I'm not surprised.

GEORGE. Then one day…this is tough to talk about.

FRED. It's okay, George.

GEORGE. One day I found myself eating seaweed.

FRED. No!

GEORGE. I realized then I had to change my life.

FRED. So you straightened out.

GEORGE. But addiction is something I will always have to deal with.

FRED. That's my point. You didn't settle. You set out to improve your life.

GEORGE. Absolutely. I wasn't born with landfill property, Fred. I started out on the outer edge of the colony. There were days when my parents could only find a shoe or a tennis ball to peck at. When I was a year old I was out on my own scavenging the leftovers of the other scavengers. I worked my tail-feathers off, Fred, and finally made it to the front of the line.

FRED. Exactly. You didn't like your life so you made a change.

GEORGE. But, understand, I only changed what I could change. I worked hard and it paid off.

FRED. So you had drive and ambition. Maybe I don't.

GEORGE. Drive and ambition have nothing to do with what you want. To become a dog will take a miracle.

FRED. *(angry)* Then maybe I need a miracle.

GEORGE. Look, Fred, don't get sore. I didn't mean to ruffle your feathers.

FRED. Well, I am upset. *(beat to calm down)* And I'm only ruffling my feathers to dry 'em out.

GEORGE. It's just that, even though I've only known you for a short time, I sense that there's a bird in there that wants to break out of its shell, to take wing and soar. But from my experience...

FRED. Yeah, I know, George, you've already told me your experience, but you better save the worldly advise. Looks like our little idyl at the beach is about to change.

*(**FRED** motions to stage right as **ANNE** enters and heads for **FRED** and **GEORGE**.)*

GEORGE. What the hell? Just when we get comfortable and get a good visit going she pops in.

*(**ANNE** stops half-way and sits.)*

At least she didn't come running and screaming at us the way the smaller ones do. Or their dogs. Wanna split?

FRED. We can just move a little.

*(**GEORGE** and **FRED** move to stage left and sit.)*

That should do it?

ANNE. I need to talk to someone.

FRED. Oh, Jesus. How about we wing it into the water? She should be gone by the time we get back.

ANNE. Naturally, I don't expect you to answer.

FRED. What the hell is she saying? Did you ever learn their ridiculous speech?

GEORGE. Tough on the ears, isn't it?

FRED. Did you know they give birth to live babies?

GEORGE. I heard about that. No shell, no protection. Barbaric, if you ask me.

FRED. Is she coming closer?

GEORGE. No, just kind of settling in, I think.

ANNE. My friend says I need to talk to a doctor, but I think I can work it out if I just hear myself, so if you just sit still for awhile...

FRED. So far, so good. She makes a move, I'm heading for deep water.

GEORGE. I'll go with you. I'm getting a tad hungry, anyway.

ANNE. I just need a little company. Feeling kind of down. You notice I just made a joke about feathers? Down, feathers? *(beat)* I'm thinking if I just talk, I might be able to figure out some stuff. Not school stuff, like arithmetic, which I was always terrible at, but life stuff, like my husband and me, I? My marriage. That kind of stuff. *(pause)* Pretty here, isn't it. The blue sky, the white sands. Nice, you know. Peaceful. *(pause)* Well, I might as well be honest with you. I haven't been happy lately. Actually, it's been for a while. I think it's because I expected Don-that's my husband-I expect Don to be the answer for all my problems, and that may have been a problem itself. In other words, I think my answer was also my problem. That's confusing, isn't it? Maybe it's because he always held himself out to be my "little problem solver," my guardian. Maybe he just didn't want to do that anymore. I don't know. Come to think of it, I don't know too much about Don. I know he's kind of quiet, maybe a tad boring, but in a manly way, you know. Strong, silent, a tad boring Donny. Always dependable. *(pause)* I just realized I wanted to talk about me and I wound up talking about Don. Isn't that odd? What do you think that means? Don't tell anyone, but it's also a little odd I'm waiting for a seagull to answer me. Ha! That's funny. *(beat)* Anywhoo, Don left me and here I sit, alone with a couple of birds, trying to figure out what happened and what to do next. I mean, our marriage started out so beautifully. Bermuda honeymoon, nice house, good friends and now poof. The honeymoon is over. Still got the house and friends. I think I still have the house. I know I still have friends. Well…one for sure. In fact, that's her over there. Sandy's her name. She is very nice, very supportive, you know. I think she's smarter than me. In fact, for all I know you guys are smarter than me. Are you two married? Never mind. *(beat)* Sandy thinks the problem is I'm dull. Do you think I'm…Never mind. I have to stop doing that. Silly me. But I am frightened, you know. I mean, what if Don decides to not come back. I can't just sit here the rest of my life talking to you guys. Not that there's anything wrong with you guys, but we don't share the same life experiences, do we? You're birds, I'm human. A very important difference and distinction, don't you agree?

GEORGE. Want to get something to eat?

FRED. Yeah, I've heard enough squawking from her to last a life time.

*(**GEORGE** and **FRED** exit. **ANNE** remains staring toward the horizon. **DON** enters.)*

End Act 1

ACT II

(SETTING: Beach)

(AT LIGHTS: **ANNE** *is seated in a beach chair.* **DON** *is standing, at times moving around the stage.)*

DON. She didn't have to leave.

ANNE. I think she felt uncomfortable.

DON. With me?

ANNE. With us.

DON. Is she going back to Jim?

ANNE. I don't know.

DON. Yes, you do.

ANNE. Depends on what you mean by "going back."

DON. To be with him.

ANNE. Stay with him?

DON. They are married.

ANNE. Then I don't know what's she's going to do.

DON. So she said nothing to you?

ANNE. She said she was going back home. She didn't say it had anything to do with Jim.

DON. I thought you said it was because she felt uncomfortable here.

ANNE. I said that's what I thought. It was conjecture.

DON. I didn't realize you engaged in conjecture.

ANNE. Is this why you came back?

DON. Pardon?

ANNE. To engage in this verbal ping-pong.

DON. No. This is an add on.

ANNE. Then why?

DON. I wanted to see how you were doing.

ANNE. I've been talking to seagulls.

DON. Are they answering?

ANNE. Not yet.

DON. That's probably a good thing.

ANNE. In that respect they aren't much different than you.

DON. That what…?

ANNE. That they don't answer me.

DON. Not true. I always answered when you asked a question.

ANNE. Did you ever, to your knowledge, ever engage in spontaneous dialogue with me?

DON. Ridiculous. Of course.

ANNE. When?

DON. Well, I can't be expected to remember such things.

ANNE. Just pick one time. I'll wait.

DON. And I won't be put on the stand to be cross-examined.

ANNE. Fair enough.

(A long silence ensues.)

Well?

(more long silence)

DON. Just before I left.

ANNE. What about it?

DON. I was spontaneous just before I left.

ANNE. You mean you spontaneously left.

DON. I mean I remember spontaneously engaging you in a dialogue.

ANNE. Go on. Refresh my memory.

DON. Aha! I remember exactly. It was at breakfast that very morning. The morning I left. I was waiting for you in the dining room so we could have breakfast. We were seated and, this stands out in my mind, we were seated and I asked what you were planning to eat. Spontaneously, I asked you that.

ANNE. And what did I say?

DON. I don't recall. Eggs probably.

ANNE. And what did you say?

DON. I don't recall.

ANNE. I do. You said nothing. You got up and went to pile up your plate with whatever you could carry. That was that. End of talking.

DON. Can't talk and eat at the same time.

ANNE. If eating is the opposite of talking, by now you should weigh a thousand pounds.

DON. Since I came back you've done nothing but attack me. Did Sandy put you up to this?

ANNE. This is not an attack. This is engaging in dialogue.

DON. I know and I don't particularly like it.

ANNE. Well, I didn't particularly like you walking out on me.

DON. I can understand that.

ANNE. How decent of you to understand that.

DON. I came back.

ANNE. We'll get to that in a moment. If you hang around long enough.

(**DON** *sits.*)

I need to know why you left.

DON. I stopped wanting to hear you.

ANNE. I was talking about…what was I talking about?

DON. It didn't matter..

ANNE. Oh, I remember. I was talking about Bermuda. The sand, the sky, the sea, the flowers of Bermuda. Do you remember Bermuda?

DON. Of course.

ANNE. Do you remember why we were there?

DON. It was a vacation.

ANNE. It was our fucking honeymoon, Don. Our honeymoon.

DON. I knew that.

ANNE. Hooray! Is that why you left? Because I was reminiscing about our honeymoon? Was it too painful for you to recall?

DON. All that seemed to matter at that moment was I needed to stop hearing you.

ANNE. Couldn't you have just asked me to be quiet?

DON. I didn't know how. It would have hurt you. *(slowly, as if befuddled)* I didn't…I didn't want to…to hurt you.

ANNE. So you thought walking out was better.

DON. Sounds weird when you put it that way.

ANNE. If you want to put it another way, I'm open. How about: it was better to walk out, you thought. No? Okay, how about better it was, you thought, to walk out. No? Then how about…?

DON. It's weird anyway the words are strung together, Anne, I know that, but that's what I needed to do. No. Make that I didn't know what else to do.

ANNE. My voice was…what? Grating, annoying, irritating, piercing, maddening, what Donny? Tell me.

(pause)

DON. I went to see Jimmy.

ANNE. You didn't answer me.

DON. Not every question has an answer, Anne. I don't know the answer to that. I'm happy I've gotten this far today.

ANNE. *(resigned)* So you went to see Jimmy

DON. When I left here, I went home, then I went to see Jim. I told him…I told him I left you because hearing you was like having staples driven into my head. You were running on…babbling…about seagulls and I just needed to get away from you, the seagulls, the sun, the beach, this whole fucking scene. Why do you talk so much?

ANNE. Because I want to share my life with someone.

(cross fade to:)

(Bare stage, two chairs. **SANDY** *and* **JIM** *move about the stage.)*

SANDY. When did you notice I was gone?

JIM. When I got home.

SANDY. Not at the hotel?

JIM. I figured you had gone home.

SANDY. I had.

JIM. Yeah, that's what I figured.

SANDY. But I wasn't here when you got home, right?

JIM. Yeah.

SANDY. But you never called to find out where I was.

JIM. But I was right, right? You were home.

SANDY. I waited two days for you to call. For all you know I might have gotten buried in one of those stupid sand traps you seem to hate so much.

JIM. I don't really hate sand traps. They add something to the game. It's just that when you're trying to lay up to the pin…

SANDY. Have we now switched from your apparent indifference to my mysterious disappearance to talking about golf? Once again.

JIM. I was just trying to explain…See, that's the problem right there.

SANDY. Sand.

JIM. Your indifference to something very important to me.

SANDY. Golf.

JIM. Right.

SANDY. These were your choices during those two days, Jimmy: You could have tried to locate me or finish out a couple more rounds of golf. And you chose…TA DA!

JIM. I knew you were okay, okay?

SANDY. HOW? HOW DID YOU KNOW? Tell me Tiger, how did you know? How did you know I didn't drown in one of those fucking water hazards?

JIM. Because if you had, one of the ground keepers would have told me, that's how.

SANDY. You are…you are without a doubt…I can't even begin to…

JIM. But when I get home do I find Sandy? No. No Sandy. No Sandy for a week. So where the hell were you?

SANDY. None of your fucking business.

JIM. Why did you leave?

SANDY. Which time?

JIM. The resort.

SANDY. No, Jim, the real question is why did I go with you in the first place. Why do I follow you around the course like some dumb lap dog when you don't give a shit if I'm there or climbing a tree? It's like a script we follow. Want to hear the script?

JIM. I know the script. Over the years you've made it quite clear what's in it. So, no, cram your script. Why weren't you home when I got there?

SANDY. Holding your newspaper, slippers and a martini?

JIM. You've never done that, ever, but it sounds like a nice change. Where were you?

SANDY. Holding Ann's hand.

JIM. While Don was here.

SANDY. Don was here?

JIM. If you were here a week ago, you'd be sitting on his lap.

SANDY. He had left Ann.

JIM. He just went back to her.

SANDY. Why?

JIM. He missed her. Is that why you came back?

SANDY. No.

JIM. Then…?

SANDY. To see if I made a mistake.

JIM. And?

SANDY. Still not sure.

JIM. So this is a test?

SANDY. In a way.

JIM. You think you can pass a test?

SANDY. Try me.

JIM. Where were you every Wednesday night? For the past year, where were you?

(**SANDY** *sits.*)

SANDY. Truth?

JIM. No, lie to me, Sandy.

SANDY. Out with the girls.

JIM. Is that the truth?

SANDY. You said I should lie to you.

JIM. You're making me crazy.

(*Cross fade to* **FRED** *and* **GEORGE.**)

FRED. I am stuffed, George.

GEORGE. Lot of fish out there, Fred. Any idea what they were?

FRED. Doesn't really matter to me, kiddo. I'll chow down whatever.

(*They squat and begin to preen.*)

GEORGE. Looks like our friend is gone.

FRED. Sometimes they come out here and lay down for seems like forever. First they smear some gunk on themselves and then just lay there. Maybe it's some strange ritual.

GEORGE. Maybe they die.

FRED. I don't think so, because they always leave.

GEORGE. Personally, I've haven't had much to do with those kind. They hardly ever show up at the landfill.

FRED. So...what were we talking about, George?

GEORGE. Generally, about you being unhappy with your lot in life. Specifically, about wanting to become a dog.

FRED. And you kind of doubting that could happen.

GEORGE. I guess nothing is impossible, but I don't think we can change like that. Seagull into dog, or dog into seagull.

FRED. You're saying I'm stuck.

GEORGE. I may not be the brightest gull in the world, Fred, but seems to me your problem isn't being a gull, but being an unhappy gull.

FRED. Exactly. The only reason I mentioned being a dog was because they seemed to have so much fun, to be able to romp and play and cavort on the beach.

GEORGE. They may cavort, but have you noticed when they leave one of the two legged things puts a rope around their necks? And sometimes they drag them off the beach.

FRED. You're right. I forgot about that.

(**FRED** *mulls as* **GEORGE** *preens.*)

So you're saying…

GEORGE. Play the cards you're dealt.

FRED. What if I can't?

GEORGE. It's just a matter of adjusting. It's like when we sit in the water. Up, down, waves, no waves, tide, no tide. We just ride it out.

FRED. I meant I can't play the cards because I have no fingers, remember. Check it out. *(displays feathers)*

GEORGE. Is that a joke?

FRED. Not very good, huh.

GEORGE. You're just trying to deflect feelings, Fred.

FRED. You're right. How'd you catch on so quickly?

GEORGE. I have a talent for this. All the gulls in the landfill come to me with their problems.

FRED. You get paid to listen?

GEORGE. I work on a sliding scale. Those that can, bring me fish. Those that can't, I carry.

FRED. You really are a nice bird, George.

GEORGE. I know. I also know you just changed the subject from you to me.

FRED. You are dangerous, George.

GEORGE. How so?

FRED. You don't let me off the hook.

GEORGE. That's my AA experience showing.

FRED. I've thought about the dog thing and I guess you're right.

GEORGE. I'm glad you've become reasonable about that.

FRED. It was being dragged by the neck that woke me up. I don't think I can deal with that.

GEORGE. Shocking to see, Fred.

FRED. So I decided to become a person.

GEORGE. I thought you understood…

FRED. Better to be the dragger than the draggee, I figure.

GEORGE. I still don't think you get the point.

FRED. Yes, I do, George. That's what I want.

GEORGE. I'm worried about you, Fred.

FRED. Thanks, but once I become a person I'm set. I've been watching them for years, George. They live in that big house over there. They hang around without much to do, have food brought to them, fresh food, by the way, lay on the beach. And they're the ones who drag the dogs. What a great life people have. I guess I'll miss being able to fly, but that's a small price to pay, right?

GEORGE. I hope you realize this is impossible.

FRED. Friends are supposed to be supportive, George.

GEORGE. I am your friend. That's why I think my being a reality check comes first. If all's clear on the reality front, then supportive can follow. As your friend, you can't expect me to support dangerous or crazy.

FRED. And which do you think I am?

GEORGE. Both, I'm afraid.

FRED. So you're saying I need to buy into your logic, that I have to buy into status quo, or I can't count on you.

GEORGE. I'm saying you're not being reasonable. Don't forget I do counselling back home.

FRED. Then maybe you should go back home, George.

GEORGE. You're telling me to leave?

FRED. I'm telling you it's a big beach, George and it runs from here all the way back to Staten Island.

GEORGE. What are you going to do?

FRED. Check into that big house over there and order some shrimp.

*(**FRED** runs off stage flapping his wings. **GEORGE** watches **FRED** for a while, then he runs off stage in the opposite direction, flapping his wings. Cross fade to **ANNE** and **DON**.)*

DON. You're saying you can't share your life with me.

ANNE. Do you realize what it's like to live with a vacuum?

DON. A little melodramatic, Anne.

ANNE. In lieu of nuance, Don, I resort to melodrama. Would you like to know what I did when you left?

DON. Yes.

ANNE. I waited for you to return. I waited a week for you to return before I called Sandy. Can we agree that is weird?

DON. I don't think I can give an answer that won't upset you.

ANNE. Oh, that's good, Donny. Very good. Now you're hiding behind wanting to not upset me. Delicate little me. How thoughtful. I want an answer. Can we agree it was weird my waiting a week for you to return?

DON. It was weird.

ANNE. Thank you.

DON. Why did…

ANNE. Because I felt I was frozen solid. As if my blood was ice. As if my brain was in the deep freeze. I became a frozen head of lettuce. I barely ate. I slept endlessly. I drank myself into a stupor. I'll bet my metabolism dropped to that of python.

DON. But then you…

ANNE. I looked out of the window and saw this seagull sitting on the beach.

DON. Yeah? So?

ANNE. The seagull was just sitting there, tranquil, minding it's own business. Just sitting. *(pause)* Then this dog… this big, stupid looking, hairy, mangy, nasty dog comes bounding onto the beach and heads right for the seagull.

DON. Is this some sort of metaphor, Anne, because…

ANNE. Shut up.

DON. Before you wanted me to talk, now you tell me to shut up.

ANNE. So the dog is after the seagull, right? Heads right for it. I could almost see its drool. The seagull runs away a few steps, the dog in hot pursuit. So the seagull simply flaps it's wings and flies away.

DON. Can I speak?

ANNE. Yes.

DON. So you want to be the seagull?

ANNE. No, you dummy. You do. I want to be the dog.

(cross fade to **JIM** *and* **SANDY***)*

SANDY. What do you think I'm doing Wednesday nights?

JIM. You're a candy striper at the hospital.

SANDY. You really think that?

JIM. I think you're seeing another guy.

SANDY. You really want to go there?

JIM. No. *(pause)* Is that what you're doing?

SANDY. Yes.

(pause)

JIM. I feel as if someone just shot me.

SANDY. You had no idea?

JIM. I don't know how to answer that.

SANDY. I should have lied.

JIM. WHO IN THEIR RIGHT MIND…

SANDY. Stop screaming.

JIM. …would admit to something like that?

SANDY. Now we're even, because I don't know how to answer that.

(pause)

JIM. Do you hate me that much?

SANDY. Too strong.

JIM. Ah! So now we are going to negotiate the degree of hate…

SANDY. And not the entire point.

JIM. …and closeness to the point, sort of like pitching horseshoes.

(pause)

SANDY. I don't hate you. But I don't love you. That's the point.

JIM. You want to leave me.

SANDY. I already have, but you never noticed.

JIM. I noticed you weren't around Wednesday evenings.

SANDY. True. Wednesdays I wasn't around physically. Every other day I wasn't around emotionally.

JIM. Why did you just go away with me, then?

SANDY. Hoping.

JIM. For what?

SANDY. That I was wrong. I wasn't wrong.

JIM. I suddenly feel very sad.

*(**SANDY** starts to move toward him.)*

I wasn't asking for your sympathy.

*(**SANDY** stops.)*

SANDY. Yes, you were and you almost had me. I stopped because I remembered how we got to this point. All those years of bad choices, all those fucking birdy wordys.

JIM. What?

SANDY. It doesn't matter any more, Jimmy.

JIM. Is this why you never wanted to have a kid with me?

SANDY. Maybe.

JIM. Even though I thought we had something once, that we could have been good parents, or at least I would have had a chance to be a decent father.

SANDY. Maybe you would have, but I had no interest in being a good, bad or any kind of mother. But as I said, it doesn't matter anymore.

(cross fade as **GEORGE** *enters)*

GEORGE. Hey, babe, you around? Ethel? You here?

*(***ETHEL** *enters.)*

ETHEL. I didn't expect you home so soon, George.

GEORGE. I wanted to get home to you, Ethel.

(Both sit, rub beaks, then preen their feathers.)

ETHEL. So how was it, George?

GEORGE. First: everything okay here?

ETHEL. Oh, yeah. Not much changes in a landfill, you know. Trucks come in, trucks go out. But I'll fill you in later. You're the one who had the adventure, mister world traveler. How was it?

GEORGE. Mixed. The place was dynamite. Beautiful beach, water so clear I never had a problem spotting food. A real nice place, Ethel. Next time we both go.

ETHEL. Missed me, huh?

GEORGE. Every minute.

(They rub beaks.)

Then there was this gull I met. Nice guy, but very disturbing.

ETHEL. Some gulls can be that way.

GEORGE. I've met some gulls who aren't happy with their lives…

ETHEL. Tell me about it.

GEORGE. You?

ETHEL. No, silly. Do I seem unhappy? I was thinking of Harvey. You remember Harvey?

GEORGE. Yeah. Sad story, but that's because Mildred was...

ETHEL. Buried by that load of trash.

GEORGE. Well, Mildred was too impatient. Couldn't wait for the truck to leave. I tell you, Ethel, life is in the timing. So of course Harvey was upset. What he needs to do is find someone else, someone like you. *(beat)* Just not you, right?

(**ETHEL** *rubs his beak.*)

ETHEL. Not to worry, mister jet setter. So, back to the unhappy gull.

GEORGE. First he wanted to be a dog. When I finally talked him out of that, he switched to becoming a person.

ETHEL. Now that is interesting.

GEORGE. I could understand wanting to be an eagle or a hawk or some other raptor, but change species entirely?

ETHEL. I could see it, though. Try a whole new life experience.

GEORGE. Well, first of all, I may not be the brightest gull...

ETHEL. Yes, you are, Georgie.

GEORGE. But I can only believe what I see and I've never seen anything change species. Have you?

ETHEL. What about Leroy a couple of years ago?

GEORGE. When he wanted to sit on Linda's egg?

ETHEL. You have to admit it was strange. And then there was the necklace thingee he found in the landfill and insisted wearing around his neck.

GEORGE. Messing around with your sexuality isn't the same as changing species, Ethel. Besides, once LeRoy met Jack, he was very happy.

ETHEL. That's true. Except he hasn't been able to figure out how to put those earrings on.

GEORGE. LeRoy is a nice guy, but a little looney, I think.

ETHEL. Oh, is that a joke?

GEORGE. No, why?

ETHEL. Never mind, George. What kind of dog did this gull want to be?

GEORGE. Didn't seem to matter. I think the real issue was he was depressed. Suicidal maybe. Seemed to run in his family.

ETHEL. What would make him depressed, George? Whether we live on the landfill or roam the beaches, we have the sky, the water, the plenty of food. Sounds good to me.

GEORGE. That's the thing, though. He didn't have someone like you.

(They rub beaks.)

Now it's your turn. What news?

ETHEL. I have an egg on the way.

(cross fade to ANNE and DON)

DON. You want to be a dog?

ANNE. Exactly.

DON. You want to be nasty and mangy and drooling and whatever else you said?

ANNE. Exactly.

DON. You want to chase me away?

ANNE. I want to feel I had some impact on your life. I want to feel that there is some rationale for you taking flight just because I talk to fill a vacuum. I want...I need to know I have...I don't know what I need to know... Wait, yes I do. I need to know I have presence. I deal with Sandy I know I have presence. I deal with my hairdresser I know I have presence. When I deal with you I feel invisible and then you become invisible and then we are both are invisible to each other. And what makes me crazy is that you don't even know it. *(pause)* Am I talking too much again? Tell me, please, tell me. I don't want you flying off again before we get this settled.

(pause)

DON. There was a point a couple of years ago when I remember looking at my parents and wondering how did they manage to stay together for so long. At that time it was, what, forty years. I couldn't understand it.

ANNE. It couldn't have been forty years. They got a divorce after thirty-eight years. I should have known then you had grounds for being strange.

DON. But they lasted thirty-eight years, Anne.

ANNE. You make it sound like a prison sentence and the divorce was a parole, time off for good behavior or something. And who gets a divorce after thirty-eight years? Did it just kind of sneak up on them? Hey, wadda ya know, we're unhappy. Or was it a long time coming? If so, how could they stand being unhappy for so long? This whole marriage thing has become very murky, Donald.

DON. Is that where we're headed?

ANNE. Divorce?

DON. Are you asking for one or just want me to explain my question?

ANNE. Explain the question.

DON. Do you think we're headed for a divorce?

ANNE. Maybe.

DON. What about our plans for a kid?

(pause)

ANNE. For that to happen, you have a lot of work to do, Donny.

*(Cross fade to **JIM** seated on a bar stool. He's holding a golf club. **DON** enters holding a drink and a golf club.)*

DON. Worst round I ever shot.

JIM. Oh, I remember worse. Remember that time in Sarasota. You were...

DON. I am going to have to listen to you giving me blow by blow of my worst playing?

JIM. Just refreshing your memory.

DON. In case I forgot, huh?

JIM. What are friends for, Donny?

DON. Sometimes I wonder, Jimmy.

(pause)

JIM. So…how'd it go with Annie?

DON. According to her, I have a lot of work to do.

JIM. I agree. If you don't fix that slice, you are never going to improve your game, man.

DON. You can't be serious, can you?

JIM. I can about serious stuff.

DON. You don't think me and Anne are serious stuff?

JIM. I do. I'm sorry about the slice joke, funny though it might be.

DON. Were you and Sandy serious stuff?

JIM. Is this going to be one of those "serious" conversations?

DON. I'd like it to be, yeah. We can get back to the golf stuff later.

JIM. I thought my marriage was serious stuff, yeah. And then it became tragic stuff. And then it went poof. Except for the alimony checks, of course. Financially it went beyond tragic. Demonic may be a better word for it.

DON. We are a couple of mooks, Jim.

JIM. Mook. What the fuck is that?

DON. A loser. That's us. Mooks.

JIM. Because of our marriages? So called.

DON. You going to get married again?

JIM. How the hell do I know? I'll tell you one thing, though. If I do, she better be able to play golf.

DON. Is that the primary issue?

JIM. It's up there, Donny, my friend. I'll tell you what I don't want. What I don't want is when I tell my wife I got a birdy wordy, I don't want her sneering at me. What I want is for my wife to appreciate what she's got.

DON. That you shot a birdy wordy.

JIM. Damn right. I'll tell you what it shows. It shows a sense of appreciation of her husband. And it shows we can share something. Isn't sharing something important the basis of marriage? At least I think so, anyway. Agree?

DON. Yeah, agree. To be able to share your life with someone who cares about it.

JIM. Let me tell you. Living with Sandy was like living in a vacuum. I would talk to her about things important to me…

DON. Golf.

JIM. …more than golf. Almost anything. Travel, sports, you name it, and she'd be out to lunch and then I'd feel invisible. Do you have any idea what that felt like? It made me feel like shit.

DON. This "invisible" thing. It's like you're talking about something, anything that at the moment is important to you.

JIM. Yeah.

DON. And it's like you're in the room alone, that the other person doesn't hear you.

JIM. Exactly, Don. Exactly. Then you've had the same feelings.

DON. No, I haven't, but I think I understand.

*(Cross fade to **MABEL**, a seagull. She is seated, preening her feathers. **FRED** enters.)*

FRED. This place taken?

MABEL. *(amused)* Not enough beach for you, huh?

FRED. I just like company. It is pretty desolate out here.

MABEL. Most beaches are. Except in the summer when all those featherless, wingless creatures show up.

FRED. They're called people.

MABEL. That right?

FRED. My dad told me. Not too many of them where I come from. Plenty of gulls, though.

MABEL. Where's that?

FRED. Staten Island landfill.

MABEL. Oh, I heard of that. Always meant to visit, never have, though.

FRED. Well, it's a haul, for sure. How about you? You from here?

MABEL. Yup. I nest just over that dune, there.

FRED. Waterfront property. Nice.

MABEL. I'm Mabel.

FRED. Fred.

MABEL. So this is a vacation?

FRED. Kind of. My father, his name was George, visited here before I hatched. About four years ago. Dad said he named me after a gull he met here. He said if I had the chance I should visit so here I am. Dad's gone now. Mother, too. Her name was Ethel.

MABEL. Mine are both gone also. Sad we gulls have such a short life span, isn't it?

FRED. Depends what you do with it, I guess, but yeah, over all I'd rather do less but be able to do it longer.

MABEL. Did you fly down by yourself?

FRED. Do you mean is there a Mrs. Fred?

MABEL. If I wanted to know if there is a Mrs. Fred, I would have asked if there is a Mrs. Fred.

FRED. Sorry. Yup, flew down solo.

MABEL. So…is there a Mrs. Fred?

FRED. Nope. Do you live by ourself?

MABEL. Do you mean is there a Mr. Mabel?

FRED. If I want to know if there is a Mr. Mabel, etc. etc.

MABEL. Touché.

FRED. Thank you. So, is there a…

MABEL. Nope. Not yet.

   (**MABEL** *looks up. Then at* **FRED**.)

   The air currents look good today. Want to take a ride?

FRED. Think you can keep up with me?

MABEL. Well, I might have to slow down a bit.

FRED. Touché back at you, Mabel.

MABEL. You ready, Fred?

FRED. Up, up and away, kiddo.

> (**MABEL** and **FRED** run off flapping their wings. Cross fade to **ANNE**. She is seated with a drink in one hand, a book in the other. **SANDY** enters.)

SANDY. It's still beautiful down here.

ANNE. Enjoy your walk?

SANDY. Lovely.

> (**SANDY** sits.)

I was watching those birds take off. Man they really get up there.

ANNE. Seagulls.

SANDY. Right. Seagulls. Filthy things.

ANNE. I find 'em comforting to watch. Look *(she points).* That one. Staring into the water. Have you ever seen anything so tranquil?

SANDY. My cat.

ANNE. Bobbie?

SANDY. Dumb cat can stare out the window for hours.

ANNE. Did you know some gulls mate for life.

SANDY. I thought that was swans.

ANNE. That's right. But some gulls, too.

SANDY. That's another reason I couldn't be a gull. Too many good looking gulls out there to get stuck with one. Then, of course, I don't think I'd look good in feathers. Time for our piña coladas?

ANNE. A little later, okay?

SANDY. How's little Jen?

ANNE. Oh, you should see her, Sandy. She…

SANDY. How old is she now?

ANNE. Three next month.

SANDY. Amazing.

ANNE. And she started nursery school.

SANDY. No.

ANNE. Honest. Half day, but she loves it. I peek in sometimes to watch her. Amazing. She has little friends and they do all these little things together and she smiles and plays. Just like a real person.

SANDY. Are you trying to make me envious?

ANNE. Not for a million dollars, Sandy. I just like to tell people what's happening, share my life, you know?

SANDY. I'm kidding, Anne. Well, I think I'm kidding. Anyway, I'm the one who asked. How long can your parents hold up baby sitting?

ANNE. They offered a week, but I expect to get a call in a couple of days. The return flight was left open.

SANDY. Look at that guy *(nods off to indicate)*. See what I mean about "for life?" What, maybe twenty-five? *(growls)*

ANNE. You're still at it, huh?

SANDY. At what?

ANNE. You used to blame it on Jim and his…birdy something or other.

SANDY. Birdy wordy. Right, I did, didn't I? Maybe the fault dear Anne lay not in the Jim, but in my loins. Well, too late now.

ANNE. Ever hear from him?

SANDY. Only when my alimony check is late and I call him. I've heard from people he found someone else. Seems she's a scratch player, whatever that is. Sounds like something you'd need a dermatologist for.

ANNE. Isn't it strange how we can have deeply felt connections one minute and then apparent total indifference the next?

SANDY. Can I respond to that one section at a time?

ANNE. Anyway you like.

SANDY. First off, you are assuming I am capable of "deeply felt connections." Second...

ANNE. Not to me either?

SANDY. I think I closed the admissions process right after high school. You were grand-fathered in. Or is that grand-mothered in? So...second, you therefore assume I had "deeply felt connections" for what's his name.

ANNE. You are terrible, Sandy. You've known him since...

SANDY. You're right. I am terrible, but damned if I know why or care to find out at this point. Thirdly, I am not totally indifferent. He was totally indifferent. If he had not been totally indifferent, we would...well, we might...who knows what? Fourthly...I am getting a lot of mileage out of this, aren't I...?

ANNE. And without liquid refreshment.

SANDY. Exactly. Don't know about you, but I'm impressed. And dry. So...fourthly, it was not a case of one minute this, next minute that. After ten years...make that eight years of trying to get his attention, I realize the futility and cut my losses.

ANNE. And during those other two years...?

SANDY. Sandy found a friend or two or three to pay close attention.

(**DON** *enters with a tray of drinks.*)

Like a faithful St. Bernard bringing brandy to the snow-bound.

DON. *(to* **SANDY***)* Notice I put two umbrellas in yours.

SANDY. *(to* **ANNE***)* Eat your heart out.

(**DON** *passes around the drinks. He stands staring out to sea.*)

DON. I'm going to walk up the beach.

SANDY. Fine with me. Just bring back a couple more of these.

ANNE. I think he was talking to me, Sandy.

SANDY. Maybe so, but I'd still like him to bring back a couple more of these.

DON. *(to* **ANNE***)* Want to come?

ANNE. Give me a minute.

(**DON** *walks away, but is in view.*)

SANDY. So, how'd you work it out?

ANNE. I'm not sure we have, but we're trying.

SANDY. I feel better not trying. It's like the relief I felt giving up trying to squeeze myself into a smaller size.

ANNE. You were always way ahead of me in understanding what you need to make you happy, Sandy. I'm just getting to it now.

SANDY. Better to have a late epiphany than no epiphany at all. So, tell me, what bulb lit for you?

ANNE. It might sound a little corny.

SANDY. I wouldn't have you any other way, Annie, or I might not recognize you.

ANNE. When you look out toward the water what do you see?

SANDY. Nothing. There's nothing there, nothing to see.

ANNE. And there never will be.

SANDY. Are we getting to some big existential moment here?

ANNE. No. Just some small recognition of what I need. And Don has come to some small recognition of what he needs. And we only find it by looking at each other.

(pause)

You okay?

SANDY. I'm fine.

ANNE. I'm going for a walk with Don.

(**SANDY** *stares out at the water. After a brief pause,* **ANNE** *joins* **DON** *and they "walk up the beach." We hear seagulls. Lights fade on* **SANDY***.*)

The End

PROPERTIES

Beach chairs (2)
Sunglasses (3)
Drinking glasses
Straws
Café table and 2 chairs

COSTUMES

ANNE: Bathing suit
Sun hat
Sandals
Beach coat

DON: Bathing suit
Sandals
Casual pants and shirt

JIM: Casual pants and shirt

SANDY: Bathing suit
Sun hat
Sandals
Beach coat
Casual dress

GEORGE, FRED, ETHEL, FRED, the younger, **MABEL:** All seagulls. Do the best you can, but the least should be a bird mask.

Also by Henry Meyerson...

Beware the Man Eating Chicken

Fresh Brewed: Tales From the Coffee Bar

Proceed to Checkout

Shtick

Please visit our website **samuelfrench.com** for complete descriptions and licensing information

www.ingramcontent.com/pod-product-compliance
Lightning Source LLC
Chambersburg PA
CBHW070650300426
44111CB00013B/2356